Read-About Holidays

El Día de los Muertos

The Day of the Dead

By Mary Dodson Wade

Consultants
Nanci R. Vargus, Ed.D.
Primary Multiage Teacher
Decatur Township Schools, Indianapolis, Indiana

Katharine A. Kane, Reading Specialist
Former Language Arts Coordinator
San Diego County Office of Education

Children's Press®
A Division of Scholastic Inc.
New York   Toronto   London   Auckland   Sydney
Mexico City   New Delhi   Hong Kong
Danbury, Connecticut

Designer: Herman Adler Design
Photo Researcher: Caroline Anderson
The photo on the cover shows a family celebrating El Día de los Muertos.

Library of Congress Cataloging-in-Publication Data

Wade, Mary Dodson.
  El Día de los Muertos / by Mary Dodson Wade.
      p. cm. — (Rookie read-about holidays)
Includes index.
Summary: Explains how Mexican families celebrate the lives of their
deceased loved ones, including sharing pictures and stories, preparing feasts,
and lighting candles in the graveyard on November 1, The Day of the Dead.
  ISBN 0-516-22493-X (lib. bdg.)   0-516-27354-X (pbk.)
  1. All Souls' Day—Mexico—Juvenile literature. [1. All Souls' Day—
Mexico. 2. Holidays—Mexico.] I. Title. II. Series.
  GT4995.A4 W33 2002
  394.266—dc21

                                    2002005489

Do you celebrate El Día de los Muertos (ehl DEE-ah deh lohs MWEHR-tohs)?

November 2004

Sunday	Monday	Tuesday	Wednesday	Thursday	Friday	Saturday
	1	2	3	4	5	6
7	8	9	10	11	12	13
14	15	16	17	18	19	20
21	22	23	24	25	26	27
28	29	30				

El Día de los Muertos,
or the Day of the Dead, is
celebrated on November 1.

People go to cemeteries
to celebrate this day.

It is a happy time, not a sad one. Families visit the graves of people they have loved.

They bring yellow
marigolds to the graves.

These flowers were special to the Aztecs (AZ-teks). The Aztecs were people who ruled Mexico a long time ago.

The Aztecs thought that a person's spirit did not die. Yellow was the special color for the spirits.

Families have picnics at the cemeteries. They eat food that their loved ones liked to eat. They drink hot chocolate.

They eat a special bread
called *pan de muerto*
(pahn deh MWEHR-toh).
Sometimes this bread has
raisins in it. The icing on
top looks like a skeleton.

Pan de Muertos

Grownups talk about the person who died. Children learn about their families and their family history.

Sometimes people bring pictures. The pictures help children remember the people who have died. People put candles on the graves.

Families stay until dark.
They sing songs that
their loved ones liked.
The candles glow in
the cemetery.

Some people stay all night near the graves of their loved ones.

Stores sell candy shaped like skulls.

Some children play with toy skeletons.

El Día de los Muertos is for families. It is a day to remember the people they have loved.

Words You Know

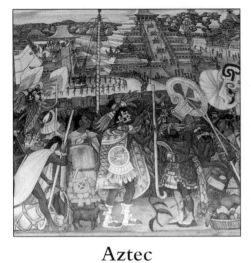

Aztec

candles

candy

cemetery

family

grave

marigolds

pan de muerto

Index

About the Author

Mary Dodson Wade loves to travel. She learns interesting things and likes to share them with others. She used to be a school librarian, but now she writes books on her computer in Houston, Texas. When she travels, a little computer goes with her.

Photo Credits

Photographs © 2002: Corbis Images: 8, 10, 13, 31 bottom left, 31 top right (Danny Lehman), 27 (Charles and Josette Lenars); D. Donne Bryant Stock Photography: 17, 31 bottom right (Stewart Aitchison), 11, 30 top left (D. Donne Bryant), 3 (R. Merkel/Latin Stock), 21, 29, 31 top left (Suzanne L. Murphy); PhotoEdit/Paul Conklin: 7, 30 bottom right; Viesti Collection, Inc./Joe Viesti: 14, 18, 22, 25, 26, 30 top right, 30 bottom left; Woodfin Camp & Associates/Robert Frerck: cover.